12 Fabulously Funny Fairy Tale Plays

by Justin McCory Martin

S C H O L A S T I C
PROFESSIONAL BOOKS

NEW YORK * TORONTO * LONDON * AUCKLAND * SYDNEY
MEXICO CITY * NEW DELHI * HONG KONG * BUENOS AIRES

To John and Sue von Brachel,
a fairy tale couple

Cover design by Kelli Thompson
Cover artwork by Terry Sirrell
Interior design by Susan M. Ragognetti
Interior artwork by Jamie Smith

ISBN: 0-439-15389-1
Copyright © 2002 by Justin McCory Martin

-Contents-

-Introduction-

Fractured fairy tales are good solid fun. Taking a familiar story and twisting it around, turning it upside down even, can truly serve to stretch your students' imaginations. This book features a dozen classic tales retold as madcap plays that can be read aloud in the classroom.

Plays are great for rainy days or anytime. Kids enjoy them and it helps build their reading confidence.

This book includes *Spiderella*, a new version of the classic "Cinderella," featuring a young spider who heads for the Bug Ball fitted out in eight tiny glass slippers. There's also such fractured fare as *The Brementown Rappers, Little Late Riding Hood, Rafunzel,* and *Goldilocks and the Three Bullfrogs*.

Performing these plays will help your students with reading, comprehension, and vocabulary development.

The plays are also meant to help unleash creativity. For example, seeing the familiar "Three Little Pigs" transformed into the fractured *Three Little Elephants* can help students to see the value of twists and surprises.

Fostering a playful imagination is one of the surest routes to creativity. In fact, some of the greatest flights of fancy are simply fractured forms of earlier versions. What is *West Side Story* if not a fractured version of *Romeo and Juliet?*

Each of the 12 plays is also accompanied by a teacher's guide. These guides include a bit of history and a plot summary of the original tales, some of which were first told by Aesop, Hans Christian Andersen, or the Brothers Grimm. To further involve your students in the tales, there are also discussion questions and writing prompts, as well as vocabulary boosters.

Enjoy these fractured fairy tales.

-Spiderella-
(based on "Cinderella")

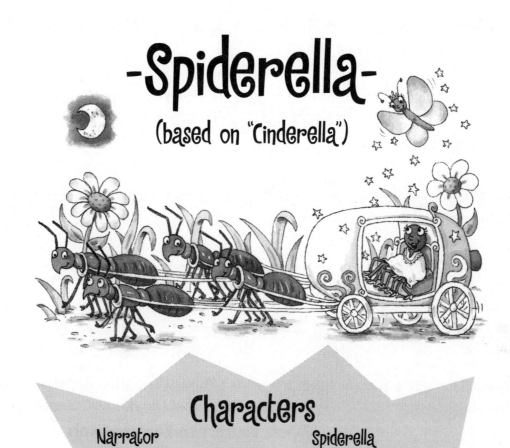

Characters

Narrator

First Ladybug Stepsister

Second Ladybug Stepsister

Spiderella

Fairy Godmoth

Cicada Prince

Narrator: Spiderella lived with her two ladybug stepsisters. The stepsisters were very mean. They were constantly making fun of Spiderella. They always made Spiderella do all the chores.

First Ladybug: We're both beautiful ladybugs. We have pretty spots and dainty wings. We have six legs. You have eight legs.

Second Ladybug: Yeah, you're weird, Spiderella. You have two extra legs. The only thing your extra legs are good for is doing housework.

First Ladybug: Hop to it, Spiderella. Put those extra legs to work. Sweep out the pantry! Clean up the kitchen!

Second Ladybug: We're ladybugs. We're too sweet and pretty to do housework. Besides, we might hurt one of our beautiful wings.

Narrator: Spiderella went about her work sadly. Her two mean ladybug stepsisters simply sat around the house chattering and gossiping. They were both very excited. There was going to be a big Bug Ball thrown by the Cicada Prince.

First Ladybug: I'm so excited. I want to look beautiful so that the Cicada Prince will fall in love with me.

Second Ladybug: I'm going to wear a lovely ball gown and the Cicada Prince will ask me to marry him.

Spiderella: I'd like to go to the Bug Ball, too.

First Ladybug: That's the craziest thing I've ever heard. You have eight legs, not six. How would you even dance?

Second Ladybug: The only thing you're good for is cleaning and spinning webs. Go spin us gowns for the ball.

Narrator: The day of the ball arrived. The cruel ladybug stepsisters set off wearing the gowns that Spiderella had spun. Spiderella stayed home dressed in ragged clothing and doing chores. Spiderella washed and dried the dishes with her eight legs. She was very sad.

Spiderella: Oh, I wish I could go to the Bug Ball. It would be so much fun.

Narrator: Spiderella was crying so hard that she didn't even notice that she had a visitor. It was a brown insect with wings and a tiny tiara. It was her Fairy Godmoth.

Fairy Godmoth: Why are you crying, Spiderella?

Spiderella: I wish I could go to the Bug Ball.

Fairy Godmoth: And you shall, my dear. I am your Fairy Godmoth and I will grant your wish. Now, Spiderella, go and fetch an acorn.

Narrator: Spiderella picked out a nice round acorn. The Fairy Godmoth flapped her wings and the acorn turned into a tiny acorn coach. It was drawn by four strong ants.

Spiderella: Thank you, Fairy Godmoth. What a wonderful way to travel to the Bug Ball. But I don't have anything to wear.

Fairy Godmoth: Don't worry, my dear. I will give you a beautiful outfit.

Narrator: The Fairy Godmoth flapped her wings. Suddenly, Spiderella's rags turned into a beautiful dress. The Fairy Godmoth flapped her wings one more time. Glass slippers appeared before Spiderella. There were eight of them, set up in a neat row. Spiderella put on the eight glass slippers and climbed into the acorn coach drawn by the four strong ants.

Spiderella: Well, I'm off to the Bug Ball.

Fairy Godmoth: Have a wonderful time, dear. But remember, be back home by the stroke of midnight. Otherwise, your acorn coach will turn back into an acorn and your gown will turn back to rags.

Narrator: At the Bug Ball, Spiderella had a wonderful time. She danced with a very handsome cricket and an extremely humorous roly-poly.

Cicada Prince: And now, I'd like to play a song for the most beautiful bug at the ball.

First Ladybug: He's walking right toward me.

Second Ladybug: You're bugging out, sis. He's obviously walking toward me.

Narrator: The Cicada Prince walked past the two ladybugs and stood directly in front of Spiderella. He began to rub his wings together and it made a lovely buzzing sound. Spiderella couldn't believe it. The Prince was playing a special song just for her. She was the bug of the ball.

Cicada Prince (crooning): You're a beautiful bug. Together we could be snug. We could live in a rug. Or inside an old jug.

Spiderella (clapping her eight legs): What a lovely song.

Cicada Prince: Thank you. Would you care to dance the jitterbug with me?

Narrator: Spiderella and the Cicada Prince danced the jitterbug. But soon, Spiderella realized that it was nearly midnight. She scurried out of the ball, moving so quickly that she lost all eight of her glass slippers. The next day, the Cicada Prince traveled around the forest trying to find the beautiful bug that had captured his heart. He brought the eight tiny glass slippers with him. If he could find who they belonged to, he would have found his love bug. He knocked on the door of the home where Spiderella and the two ladybugs lived.

First Ladybug: Who is it? Who is it?

Second Ladybug: It's the Cicada Prince.

First Ladybug: Well, open the door.

Cicada Prince: Good afternoon, ladybugs.

First Ladybug: Hello, Prince. Can I get you a lump of sugar to chew on?

Second Ladybug: Hello, Prince. Can I get you a glass of bug juice?

Cicada Prince: No thank you, ladybugs. But I do have a favor to ask. Can each of you try on these glass slippers?

Narrator: The first ladybug stepsister tried on a glass slipper. But it was too small and didn't fit. But the second ladybug found that the slippers fit just fine.

First Ladybug: There, I've put on all six slippers. I am your true love. Now give me a big fat cicada kiss.

Cicada Prince: Not so fast. There are eight slippers, not six.

First and Second Ladybugs: Eight slippers!

Narrator: Just then, the Cicada Prince noticed Spiderella. Spiderella looked rather familiar. He asked her to try on the glass slippers. They fit and she had the right number of legs, eight. He'd found his love bug.

Cicada Prince: It's you. You are the beautiful bug from the ball. I love you. Say you'll be my little spider wife.

Spiderella: Of course I will, my prince. But I'd like to get rid of these glass slippers. They're really hard to walk around in.

Narrator: And so Spiderella and the Cicada Prince lived happily ever after. The Cicada Prince would often rub his wings together and sing silly songs, and Spiderella always either went barefoot or wore sneakers.

★the end★

Teacher Page

History of the Tale

Spiderella is based on "Cinderella," a fairy tale popularized by Jacob and Wilhelm Grimm, better known as the Brothers Grimm. They were German storytellers who lived during the 1800s. In the original, Cinderella is forced to do the bidding of two cruel stepsisters. They attend a ball thrown by a prince and Cinderella is left behind to do chores. Cinderella's fairy godmother appears. She waves her wand, creating a pair of glass slippers for Cinderella and transforming a pumpkin into a carriage.

Cinderella attends the ball and she and the Prince fall in love. But as in *Spiderella*, Cinderella must be home by midnight. She races out of the ball, leaving a glass slipper behind. The next day, the Prince travels through the countryside searching for the owner of the glass slipper. He discovers that it fits Cinderella, and they live happily ever after.

Vocabulary Boosters

This story contains several words that may be new to your class:

dainty (adj.): delicate and pretty

pantry (noun): a small room, used for storing food

tiara (noun): a crown worn to special occasions, such as balls

Discuss these words with your students and invite them to use each in a sentence.

Discussion Starters

◎ Spiderella had a Fairy Godmoth. Ask students what they would do if they had a Fairy Godmother. What wish would they want granted?

◎ The two Ladybug Stepsisters were unfair toward Spiderella. Ask your students if they have encountered situations in which they were treated unfairly. What is the best way to respond in such situations?

Writing Prompts

◎ The original fairy tale "Cinderella" features a ball. Spiderella features a Bug Ball. Dream up a strange party and write about it. It can be a zoo formal with all the penguins in tuxedos. Or it could be a dinosaur dance! Have fun and let your imagination run wild.

◎ Because spiders have eight legs, Spiderella had to wear eight tiny glass slippers. What are some other things fairy tale spiders might have to wear—pants with eight legs? How would a spider ride a bicycle? Would it catch a ball using its web? Write a fairy tale about a spider, and remember: everything that you do with two arms and two legs, a spider has to do with eight legs.

-The Emperor's New Hair-

(based on "The Emperor's New Clothes")

Characters

Narrator   Mr. Twee
Emperor   Imperial Hairdresser
Traveling Salesperson   Townspeople
Mr. Twiddle   Little Boy

Narrator: Once there was a very powerful emperor. He ruled over a huge land. But there was something that he was secretly embarrassed about. He didn't have one single hair on his head.

The Emperor felt that he needed to wear wigs. He had more than a hundred of them in a special closet. They were the finest wigs and could easily be mistaken for real hair.

One day a traveling salesperson showed up at the Emperor's castle with a very unusual product.

Emperor: What are you selling today? Make it quick, because I have a huge empire to run.

Salesperson: Oh, great Emperor, I have traveled here today with an amazing new product.

I want to offer you the very first batch. It's called Hair Today Magic Potion. It's just $19.99. And wait! That's not all! If you buy Hair Today Magic Potion, I will also throw in a free comb.

Emperor (touching his wig): Why would I need it? As you can see, I have a full head of hair.

Salesperson: Yes, your hair is very nice indeed. But perhaps you have a friend who could use this potion. I used to be bald myself. And as you can see, I grew plenty of new hair thanks to Hair Today Magic Potion.

Emperor: I'll take a hundred bottles. It's for my bald friend, of course.

Narrator: The Emperor began using Hair Today Magic Potion. Each night before he went to bed, he'd take off his wig and put three drops on his very shiny head.

Each morning, he'd talk to his two advisors, Mr. Twiddle and Mr. Twee. They were the only people the Emperor trusted. He'd ask them if the Hair Today Magic Potion was working.

Mr. Twiddle and Mr. Twee wanted to make the Emperor happy. They wanted to keep their jobs. So they told the Emperor what they believed he wanted to hear.

Emperor: What do you think, my trusted advisors, Twiddle and Twee? Do you think the potion is working?

Twiddle: Oh, I do. I definitely notice a difference.

Twee: Yes, you are starting to grow just a few hairs.

Emperor: Only a few?

Twee: Well, when I say a few, I mean, like, maybe twenty.

Twiddle: Or maybe fifty. They're very nice-looking hairs, I might add.

Emperor: Yes. I see them, too.

Narrator: The Emperor continued to use the potion. And his two trusted advisors continued to tell him that the potion was working. As the days went by, they began to tell more and more extravagant lies to the Emperor. Soon they even began to believe the lies themselves.

Emperor: Tell me, trusted advisors, how do I look today? Is the potion working yet?

Twiddle: Is it working? Are you kidding? You have grown a thick head of beautiful hair.

Twee: Yes, your hair is thick and straight and brown…

Twiddle: Well, I would say it's more wavy than straight. And it's more golden than brown.

Twee: But you have a lot of it. It's thick, no question.

Twiddle: Yes, you can throw away your wigs. You don't need them anymore.

Twee: In fact, if I do say so myself, Emperor, you need a haircut.

Emperor: A haircut! How wonderful. My hair is long and thick and black and curly.

Twee: Actually, it's golden and wavy.

Emperor: So it is. It's long and thick and golden and wavy.

Twiddle: And shiny.

Emperor: And shiny. It's long and thick and golden and wavy and shiny, and I need a haircut. Fetch me the imperial hairdresser at once.

Narrator: Twiddle and Twee ran off to find the imperial hairdresser. When they found the hairdresser, they described the Emperor's new hair in great detail.

By now, they were so caught up in their lie that they completely believed it themselves. And soon, they had the imperial hairdresser convinced that the Emperor had long thick golden wavy hair that needed to be cut.

Imperial Hairdresser: Oh, Emperor, what a fine head of hair you have.

Emperor (blushing): Thank you, thank you. Right now, there's a bit too much of it. It's just a little too long and thick and golden and wavy and shiny.

Imperial Hairdresser: It will be a pleasure to trim it. I will make you look fabulous!

Narrator: The imperial hairdresser set to work with scissors and a comb. The haircut required many hours of snipping and clipping and fussing and worrying and blow-drying. But at last, the imperial hairdresser was finished.

Imperial Hairdresser: Well, what do you think?

Emperor: Maybe just a little more off the back.

Narrator: The imperial hairdresser carefully clipped the scissors near the back of the Emperor's head.

Imperial Hairdresser: Now what do you think?

Emperor: Perfect!

Twiddle: What a great style!

Twee: Everyone in the kingdom will want to get the same haircut.

Imperial Hairdresser: You look fabulous, Emperor, absolutely fabulous!

Twiddle: We should have a parade to show off your new hairstyle.

Twee: Yes, it will be inspiring for the people to see an emperor with hair that's so long and thick and golden and wavy and shiny.

Narrator: And so Twiddle and Twee arranged an elaborate parade. There were jugglers and soldiers and horses. At the tail end of the parade, the Emperor marched proudly. He wasn't wearing his crown. He wanted everyone to gaze at his wonderful new hairstyle.

    As he passed through his empire, Twiddle, Twee, and the imperial hairdresser called out to the townspeople.

Twiddle: Everyone, behold the Emperor's new hair.

Twee: Look at how golden it is! Look at how thick it is!

Imperial Hairdresser: The Emperor looks fabulous! Have you ever seen such fabulousness?

Townspeople: The Emperor's hair is long and thick and golden and wavy.

Little Boy: He doesn't have any hair.

Townspeople: And shiny! The Emperor's hair is very shiny.

Little Boy (slightly louder): He doesn't have any hair!

Townspeople (begin to chant): The Emperor's hair is fabulous! The Emperor's hair is fabulous! The Emperor's hair is fabulous!

Little Boy (loudly): Can't you people see? The Emperor doesn't have a hair on his head!

Townspeople (gasping): The Emperor doesn't have any hair!

Twiddle, Twee, Imperial Hairdresser: The Emperor doesn't have any hair!

Emperor: I don't have any hair!

Narrator: At first, the Emperor was embarrassed. But he was also glad that someone was honest enough to tell him. He called for the little boy to come out of the crowd.

Emperor: Little boy, you were the only one who was brave enough to tell me the truth.

Little Boy: Well, you are still very handsome, Emperor. You look cool without any hair.

Emperor: Thank you. That's very kind.

Narrator: The Emperor asked the little boy to walk beside him in the parade. The little boy became a trusted advisor and true friend to the Emperor. The Emperor stopped using magic hair-growth potions. He gave away his wigs to a family of traveling circus clowns.

From that point forward, the Emperor worked to run his empire kindly and wisely. No one cared that he didn't have any hair. In fact, most people thought he looked quite handsome. Twiddle and Twee even shaved their heads to look just like the Emperor.

★the end★

-Teacher Page-

History of the Tale

The Emperor's New Hair is based on "The Emperor's New Clothes" by Hans Christian Andersen. Andersen was a Danish writer who lived during the nineteenth century (1805-1875). Among his other famous stories are "The Ugly Duckling" and "The Princess and the Pea."

The fractured version of "The Emperor's New Clothes" and the original share the same themes. In both, everyone is afraid to tell the Emperor the truth. But a little boy speaks up and is rewarded for his honesty.

Vocabulary Boosters

This story contains several words that may be new to your class:

emperor (noun): the leader of a kingdom or a large territory

batch (noun): a group or set of things

extravagant (adj.): extreme

Discuss these words with your students and invite them to use each in a sentence.

Discussion Starters

◎ In The Emperor's New Hair (and in the original), matters get out of hand when people are afraid to tell the truth. Is it important to tell the truth?

◎ Can telling the truth also be dangerous? Ask your students if it's possible to get into trouble by telling someone the truth. How does one decide when to tell the truth and when to spare someone's feelings?

Writing Prompts

◎ This story features something called Hair Today Magic Potion. What if you could create your own magic potion? What would you call it and what would it do? Create an advertisement that describes the benefits of your potion.

◎ Create your own fractured version of "The Emperor's New Clothes." Use one of the following three ideas: The Emperor's New Car, The Emperor's New Pizza, The Emperor's New Shoes.

-The Brementown Rappers-

(based on "The Brementown Musicians")

Characters

Narrator   Dog/Fun-Luvin' Dawg

Donkey/Donkey MC   Cat/Kitty-O

Rooster/Da Roosta

Narrator: Once upon a time, there was a donkey who lived on a farm. He was getting old, so the farmer told him it was time to retire. The donkey had always dreamed of being a rapper. So he decided to run away to Brementown to try to make it in the music business.

   He walked along the road for a while and came upon an old hound dog.

Donkey: How are you doing?

Dog: Not so well, not so well. I'm tired of living out here in the middle of nowhere.

Donkey: You should come with me. I'm on the way to Brementown. I'm going to become a rapper.

Dog: I'd love to come along.

Donkey: Hey, I have an idea. If we're going to be rappers, we should start talking real cool. And we need new rapper names. I'll be Donkey MC.

Dog: I hear you, my donkey. From now on, you can call me Fun-Luvin' Dawg.

Narrator: The donkey and the dog continued to walk down the road. Only now they were Donkey MC and Fun-Luvin' Dawg.

   And they had cool new walks now, too. The donkey used to walk in a slow, tired way. Now Donkey MC galloped like a prize stallion. The old hound dog used to drag his belly on the ground. But Fun-Luvin' Dawg walked in a sly way, like a fox.

   Soon the two friends met up with a mangy old cat with messy fur and drooping whiskers.

Donkey MC: How's it going, my fine feline friend?

Fun-Luvin' Dawg: Yo, cat. Can I get a me-ooooow!

Cat: What is with you two? You're acting weird.

Donkey MC: We're going to Brementown. We're going to become rappers.

Fun-Luvin' Dawg: This is your chance to be a cool cat.

Cat: That sounds fun. I'm certainly not enjoying being a farm cat. The farmer says I'm getting too old. I'd love to visit Brementown.

Donkey MC: Come along with us, then. But first you have to think of a cool rapper name.

Cat: From now on, you can call me Kitty-O.

Narrator: The three animals walked down the road. The cat had a new walk now, too. Instead of being a scurrying furball, Kitty-O started to slink like a tiger.

   Pretty soon, the animals ran into a rooster.

Donkey MC: How's it crowing, my fine feathered friend?

Fun-Luvin' Dawg: Yo, rooster. Can I get a cock-a-doodle-doooo?!

Kitty-O: What's up?

Rooster: What is wrong with you? You three are acting really, really weird.

Donkey MC: We're going to Brementown. We're going to become rappers.

Fun-Luvin' Dawg: This is your chance to strut your stuff.

Kitty-O: Hey-o.

Rooster: That sounds fun. The farmer says I'm getting too old to wake him up with my crowing. He just bought a new alarm clock. I'll show him!

Donkey MC: Come along with us, then, but first you have to give yourself a cool rapper name.

Rooster: From now on, you can call me Da Roosta.

Narrator: The four animals continued down the road. Now the rooster also had a new walk. Instead of lurching awkwardly around the farmyard, Da Roosta walked with a proud strut, like a peacock.

But it was a long way to Brementown. Soon night was falling. The animals were growing tired and hungry.

There was a house in the distance with lights on. The animals walked up to the house. There were robbers sorting through their loot. Spread out on the table was all kinds of delicious food.

Donkey MC: Yo, check out those hoodlums.

Fun-Luvin' Dawg: Let me at 'em.

Da Roosta: They're going to regret the day they met Da Roosta.

Kitty-O: I'm hungry!

Donkey MC: Hush. I got a plan.

Narrator: Donkey MC's plan was to make up a rap song. The animals practiced in a whisper so that the robbers couldn't hear them.

Donkey MC: Okay, home animals, let's rap on three, and real loud. One . . . two . . . three.

Donkey MC, Fun-Luvin' Dawg, Kitty-O, Da Roosta (loudly):
> Yo, yo, we come from da farm
> And it's cause for alarm
> We're the animal crew
> And we're here to tell you
>
> If you're a robber or crook
> You're just no good in our book
> You best run home to your mamas
> And put on your pajamas

Narrator: The robbers were startled by four farm animals rapping very loudly. They ran out of the house in a fright. After they were gone, the animals went inside and feasted on the food and slept in the beds.

The next day, they walked into Brementown. When they arrived, they were surprised to learn that they were heroes. People had heard about how they scared away the robbers.

The four animals were immediately given a record contract. They made a video that played on MTV and also on various nature channels. They even went on tour with a group of robots who had formed a heavy metal band.

The Brementown Rappers went on to have five number-one songs. Here's one of their biggest hits:

Donkey MC, Fun-Luvin' Dawg, Kitty-O, Da Roosta:
> Who let the Donkey out?
> Bray, bray, bray!
> Who let the Hound out?
> Bark, bark, bark!
> Who let the Cat out?
> Purr, purr, purr!
> Who let the Rooster out?
> Crow, crow, crow!

★the end★

-Teacher Page-

History of the Tale

The original story was "The Brementown Musicians," told by the Brothers Grimm. It also features a donkey, dog, cat, and rooster. They are tired of life on the farm and feel underappreciated by their owners. The four set off to Brementown to make their fortunes as musicians. Along the way, they encounter a band of robbers. They scare them off with their singing.

The fractured version differs by having the animals become rappers. Another twist: they become famous recording artists, whereas the original Brementown musicians merely lived happily ever after.

Vocabulary Boosters

This story contains several words that may be new to your class:

feline (adj.): 1) belonging to the broad cat family, which includes lions and tigers as well as house cats 2) catlike in style and behavior

slink (verb): to move in a careful, sneaky way

loot (noun): stuff of value, usually stolen

Discuss these words with your students and invite them to use each in a sentence.

Discussion Starters

◎ Before they became rappers, the four animals were not respected on their farms. The farmers thought they were too old. Ask your students if they have encountered similar situations, in which other people did not believe in their abilities. What kinds of things can be done to shake things up? Is it good to try something new like the Brementown Rappers did?

◎ The four animals adopted nicknames when they became rappers. Inquire whether any of the students have nicknames. Do they like them? What's the secret to coming up with a good nickname?

Writing Prompts

◎ Think of some other rapper names for various animals. Write down rap songs these animals might sing.

◎ The story featured rapping farm animals. Imagine a different kind of animal adventure. Maybe a group of animals could form a football team or put on a play. Write about their adventure.

-The Three Little Elephants-

(based on "The Three Little Pigs")

Characters

Narrator

Big Bad Mouse

First Little Elephant

Second Little Elephant

Third Little Elephant

James the Butler

Narrator: Once upon a time, there were three little elephants who lived with their parents. When the elephants grew old enough, they went out into the world to live on their own.

The first little elephant built a small wooden shack. One day, there was a knock at the door.

Big Bad Mouse: Knock, knock, knock.

First Elephant: Who's there?

Big Bad Mouse (in a tiny Voice): It's the Big Bad Mouse. Open up at once!

First Elephant (can't hear the mouse): Hello? Is anybody out there?

22

Big Bad Mouse (in a tiny voice): Let me in, let me in, let me in.

First Elephant (mutters to self): That's strange. Someone knocked on my door. But whoever it was, they seem to have gone away.

Narrator: The Big Bad Mouse was frustrated. So he wrote a note and slipped it under the elephant's door. It read:

>Squeak, squeak, squeak. I'm the Big Bad Mouse.
>I'll rip up your garden. I'll tear down your house.
>I'll tug on your tail. I'll pull on your ears.
>I'm mighty and mean. I'm the worst of your fears.

Later that day the elephant found the note.

First Elephant (reading the note): A Big Bad Mouse! Oh, no. I've never seen a mouse. But it sounds very scary. I imagine that it must be giant, much larger than an elephant. I'll bet it has big yellow eyes and long sharp teeth.

Oh, no! Help! There's a Big Bad Mouse on the loose! I must run away before it comes back to my house! I must run for my life!

Narrator: The elephant ran through the wooden shack, tripping over tables and bumping into chairs. The terrified elephant left through the back door and ran all the way to the second elephant's house.

The second elephant lived in a brick house. It was larger than the first elephant's wooden shack. It also had a doorbell, which the first elephant rang. Ring, ring!

Second Elephant: Hello? Who's there?

First Elephant: It's me. I am so scared. There's a mouse on the loose. Can I stay at your house? Please, please!

Second Elephant: A mouse! I've never seen a mouse. But it sounds very scary. I imagine that a mouse must be gigantic with a long tail and sharp claws. Come inside quickly and lock the door behind you.

Narrator: A few minutes passed. The two elephants sat in frightened silence. Suddenly, the doorbell rang.

The two elephants looked at each other and their terror grew. Who could it be?

First Elephant: I'm not answering it.

Second Elephant: Don't look at me. I'm not answering it either.

Narrator: The Big Bad Mouse kept ringing the bell, but no one answered. Finally, he grew frustrated and slipped a note under the door. It read:

Squeak, squeak, squeak. I'm the Big Bad Mouse.

I'll rip up your garden. I'll tear down your house.

I'll tug on your tail. I'll pull on your ears.

I'm mighty and mean. I'm the worst of your fears.

Second Elephant (reading note): Oh, no! This is terrifying! Now the Big Bad Mouse has come to my house.

First Elephant: Oh, no! What will we do? Where will we go?

Second Elephant: There's a gigantic, frightening, fierce mouse on the loose. Run! We must run for our lives!

Narrator: The two terrified elephants stumbled out of the house, tangling up their legs, and tripping over one another. They left through the back door of the house. They didn't stop running until they arrived at the third elephant's house.

The third elephant lived in an enormous mansion. It had a long driveway and a swimming pool.

The two elephants rang the doorbell and James the Butler answered. As soon as he opened the door, they ran past him, shouting and waving their arms wildly.

First Elephant (out of breath): Oh, my! Oh, no! It's horrible! It's terrifying!

Second Elephant (out of breath): Help us! Do something! Call for help! Call the police! Call the army!

Third Elephant: Get ahold of yourselves, both of you. Now slow down and tell me what you're so frightened of.

First Elephant and Second Elephant: A mouse!

Third Elephant: A mouse?! Why didn't you say so! I've never seen a mouse. But I imagine a mouse would be humongous, larger than this mansion. I think it might have scales and it might breathe fire.

Narrator: The three elephants huddled in fear. They remained very still, listening with extreme care.
After a few minutes, the doorbell rang.

Third Elephant: Don't answer it, James.

James: Why not, Master Elephant?

Third Elephant: It's a mouse, James! A humongous, terrifying, scaly, fire-breathing mouse!

James: Don't be ridiculous. Mice are tiny furry creatures that scurry about and eat seeds and berries.

Narrator: James went and opened the door. The three elephants were so frightened now that their eyes were popping out and their ears stood straight out from their heads.

James: Well, what have we here? A little tiny mouse.

Big Bad Mouse (in a tiny voice): Would you please deliver a message to the elephants? Please tell them:
Squeak, squeak, squeak. I'm the Big Bad Mouse.
I'll rip up your garden. I'll tear down your house.
I'll tug on your tails. I'll pull on your ears.
I'm mighty and mean. I'm the worst of your fears.

James: Elephants. Come here. You must face your foe. I must say, he is not especially scary.

Narrator: The three elephants walked very nervously toward the door. The first and second elephants were looking over the shoulder of the third elephant.

The three frightened elephants stared at the doorway, but no one appeared to be there besides James the Butler. They looked to the left. They looked to the right. They looked up. Then they looked down.

There, on the doorstep, stood a little tiny mouse.

First Elephant: But you're so small!

Second Elephant: We've never seen a mouse before.

Third Elephant: You're really not very frightening at all.

Mouse (in a tiny voice): You're so huge. I did not know that this is the way you looked. You're very, very frightening. Eeeek, elephants!

Narrator: And with that, the mouse scampered into the woods. At last, the elephants had seen that a mouse was very small. They were never frightened of mice again. At last the mouse had learned that elephants are very large. The mouse never again threatened to rip up an elephant's garden or tear down an elephant's house. Everyone lived happily ever after.

★the end★

-Teacher Page-

History of the Tale

"The Three Little Pigs" is a traditional folktale. The tale was passed along for many years by oral tradition before anyone bothered to write it down. Even so, there is no definitive telling, credited to an author such as Hans Christian Andersen. Instead, a huge variety of versions are to be found in various collections of children's stories. But most versions agree on the major points. Three little pigs are harassed by a big bad wolf. The wolf blows down a straw house and a house of sticks before the pigs are able to find safety in a brick house. By contrast, this fractured version presents three elephants harassed by one very small mouse. They move to larger and larger houses until they are forced to confront the object of their terror.

Vocabulary Boosters

This story contains several words that may be new to your class:

fierce (adj.): very tough and very mean

humongous (adj.): very, very large

foe (noun): an enemy

Discuss these words with your students and invite them to use each in a sentence.

Discussion Starters

◎ Elephants are rumored to be afraid of mice. Do you think this is true? Do you have any ideas or theories about why an elephant would be afraid of such a small creature?

◎ In the story, three huge elephants are afraid of one tiny mouse. But once they actually see the mouse, they aren't scared anymore. Do you think that people often behave in a similar fashion? Are people often scared of things that they don't understand?

Writing Prompts

◎ In the story, the three elephants lived in three different types of houses – a small wooden shack, a large brick house, and a mansion. What types of things do you think would be inside an elephant's home? Choose one of the three houses from the story and describe it in detail.

◎ Everything is the opposite in this fractured fairy tale. The elephants are big and frightened. The mouse is small and brave. Write a story full of opposites: tiny mountains, huge raindrops, friendly wolves, or mean bunnies.

-The Popsicle Boy-

(based on "The Gingerbread Man")

Characters

Narrator

Little Baby

Popsicle Boy

Jump-Rope Girl

Boy on Bike

Dog

Narrator: It was the middle of a very hot summer. Each day, Mr. Cone parked his ice cream truck near a busy playground. Kids were everywhere. They loved to buy ice cream and other treats from Mr. Cone's truck.

One day, a woman asked for an orange Popsicle for her little baby. Mr. Cone reached into his freezer and pulled one out. To everyone's surprise, just as Mr. Cone was handing the Popsicle to the lady, it started to move. It was Popsicle Boy! Popsicle Boy wriggled free, jumped down from the truck, and started to run away.

Little Baby (crying and reaching out): Wah, wah, mine. My pasittle. My pasittle. Wah, wah.

Popsicle Boy: You can whimper and whine till you're 103.

I'm the Popsicle Boy and you'll never catch me.

Narrator: The Popsicle Boy began to run through the playground. A girl who was jumping rope saw him and licked her lips hungrily.

Jump-Rope Girl: It's my lucky day! I'm tired from jumping rope. But here comes an orange Popsicle running right toward me.

Narrator: Popsicle Boy was running very fast now and he ran right past the jump-rope girl.

Jump-Rope Girl: Wait! Stop! It's so hot, and you look so cool and tasty.

Popsicle Boy: You can jump double Dutch till you're 103.
  I'm the Popsicle Boy and you'll never catch me.

Narrator: There was a boy riding his bike around the playground. He was hot and tired, too. When he saw Popsicle Boy he was sure he could catch him on his bike.

Boy on Bike: That has to be the fastest-moving Popsicle I have ever seen. But it's also my favorite flavor—orange. There's no way he can outrun my bike.

Narrator: By now, Popsicle Boy was streaking through the playground at tremendous speed. The boy on the bike could not keep up.

Boy on Bike (pedaling hard): Wait! Hold on! No fair! It's so hot, and you look delicious!

Popsicle Boy: You can pedal around till you're 103.
  I'm the Popsicle Boy and you'll never catch me.

Narrator: Popsicle Boy had run almost to the end of the playground. Suddenly, he was spotted by a dog. The dog began to chase after Popsicle Boy.

Dog: Woof, woof, woof! Woof, woof, woof!

Narrator: The dog got the closest to Popsicle Boy of anyone. In fact, the dog got close enough to take one big slurp. But then even the dog could not keep up. It stopped running and started to pant underneath the hot sun.

Dog: Pant, pant, pant. Pant, pant, pant.

Popsicle Boy: You can slobber and howl till you're 103.
   I'm the Popsicle Boy and you'll never catch me.

Narrator: Popsicle Boy had outrun everyone in the playground: the little baby, the jump-rope girl, the boy on the bike, and the dog. He was free at last.
   He walked through the city for a while. Then he got on a bus. He rode out to the beach, where he lay down in the sand.

Popsicle Boy: I will lie on this beach till I'm 103.
   I'm the Popsicle Boy. No one will ever catch me.

Narrator: Popsicle Boy lay on the beach. The hot sun beat down on him. For a while, he enjoyed it. He thought perhaps he'd get a good tan. But then he began to notice that something very strange was happening to him.

Popsicle Boy: Please, oh, please. Somebody help me!
   I'm the Popsicle Boy and I'm melting quickly.
   Oh, me, oh, my. Won't someone save me!
   I'm a Popsicle Boy. I'll be wasted, you see!

Narrator: All afternoon, the sun kept shining brightly. All afternoon, Popsicle Boy melted away. By the end of the day, all that was left of him was his stick, which was stuck in the middle of a bright orange pool.

★the end★

Teacher Page

History of the Tale

"The Gingerbread Man" is another traditional fairy tale, like "The Three Little Pigs." In the original, the Gingerbread Man jumps out of a pan and runs away. He runs past a cow and a farmer. Each chases after him, hoping to catch him and eat him. But he escapes, saying, "You can't catch me, I'm the Gingerbread Man." But then the Gingerbread Man meets up with a fox who offers to help him cross a river. The fox tricks the Gingerbread Man and eats him instead. In this version, Popsicle Boy outruns everyone at the playground: the baby, the girl jumping rope, the boy on the bike, and the dog. But Popsicle Boy also gets tricked. He lies down on the beach and gets melted by the sun.

Vocabulary Boosters

This story contains several words that may be new to your class:

whine (Verb): to complain in a childish way

streak (Verb): to move very fast

pant (Verb): to breathe quickly when one is tired or worn out

Discuss these words with your students and invite them to use each in a sentence.

Discussion Starters

◎ The Popsicle Boy outran everyone at the playground. But then he melted and was wasted. Did he make a mistake? Does this story teach any lessons about the importance of being true to oneself?

◎ What if different food items could talk? Ask your students what types of personalities different foods would have. Would onion rings be fun and acrobatic? Would green beans be serious and boring?

Writing Prompts

◎ The Popsicle Boy always speaks in rhyme. Use the same style and have Popsicle Boy tell his life story. Who were his mother and father? Maybe they were ice cream cones. And what are his favorite snacks? Remember to write Popsicle Boy's story in rhyming verse.

◎ Popsicle Boy is the story of a snack that tries to escape. Write your own story about a runaway food item. It can be anything, such as a pizza boy or a doughnut girl. Have fun and let your imagination run wild!

-The Little Red Robin-

(based on "The Little Red Hen")

Characters

Narrator
Little Red Robin
Lazy Dog

Lazy Cat
Lazy Duck

Narrator: Once there was a Little Red Robin. Her favorite food in the whole wide world was a banana split with hot fudge and nuts and whipped cream and a bright red cherry on top. She decided to make a banana split. And she tried to convince her lazy friends—Dog, Cat, and Duck—to help her.

Little Red Robin: I'm in the mood for a delicious banana split. Who will go to the store with me to buy bananas and ice cream and hot fudge and nuts and whipped cream and cherries?

Lazy Dog: Are you kidding?

Lazy Cat: Not me, I need to spend the day washing my hair.

Lazy Duck: Since you're going to the store, here's five dollars. Could you pick me up a copy of *Duck Style* magazine?

Little Red Robin: Well, I guess I'll have to go to the store all by myself.

Narrator: So the Little Red Robin hopped over to the Bargain Barn grocery store. When she returned home she realized that she had forgotten to buy an important ingredient: cherries.

Little Red Robin: Oh, dear, I forgot the cherries. Will someone go back to the store with me, just to keep me company?

Lazy Dog: Are you bonkers? Can't you see I'm busy chasing my own tail?

Lazy Cat: Are you kidding? Can't you see that I'm busy playing with this piece of yarn?

Lazy Duck: Since you're going back to the store, here's ten bucks. Could you pick me up some eye drops, a bar of soap, a pack of playing cards, some garbage bags, tissues.…

Narrator: The Little Red Robin returned to the Bargain Barn grocery store. She bought cherries and also eye drops, soap, and the other items the Lazy Duck had asked for. Then she returned home and prepared to make a banana split. Once again, she asked her friends if they would help.

Little Red Robin: Who will help me to make a banana split?

Lazy Dog: I'll help if you want to whip up a batch of dog biscuits.

Lazy Cat: I'll help if you open a can of cat food.

Lazy Duck: Do you think you could go pick up my laundry by any chance?

Narrator: So the Little Red Robin proceeded to make the banana split all by herself. She cut up bananas. She scooped out lots of ice cream. Then she poured on the hot fudge and sprinkled the nuts.

Carefully following the instructions in her *Dessert Treats for the Birds* cookbook, the Little Red Robin added a heaping helping of whipped cream. And to top it all off, she added a bright red cherry. The banana split was ready.

Little Red Robin: Now I'm finished making my favorite dessert in the whole wide world, a banana split.

Lazy Dog: Hey, that looks delicious. Can I have a bite?

Lazy Cat: Mmm. That looks really good. Can I lick the spoon?

Lazy Duck: That looks great. Hey, Red Robin, can you go up to my room and find my favorite bowl? You know, the blue bowl with the stars on it. I think I'd like to have a nice big helping of that banana split.

Little Red Robin: Now I'm willing to share my banana split with all of you. But you made me do all the work by myself, which isn't fair. Next time, I want each of you to help out.

Narrator: So the Little Red Robin shared the banana split and the other three animals enjoyed it very much. The next day, Lazy Dog, Lazy Cat, and Lazy Duck surprised the Little Red Robin by making her a delicious chocolate cake. The dog, cat, and duck weren't lazy anymore. And the four friends lived happily ever after.

★the end★

Teacher Page

History of the Tale

The original tale is "The Little Red Hen." The Little Red Hen tries to persuade her lazy friends—Dog, Cat, and Duck—to help make some bread. She can't convince them to help with the planting or gathering of wheat or with the baking. But when it comes time to eat the bread, they are ready to help. Because she had to do all the work by herself, the Little Red Hen decides she will also eat the bread by herself. In this fractured version, the Little Red Robin tries to convince Dog, Cat, and Duck to help her prepare a banana split. In contrast to the original tale, she shares her dessert with the other animals, but also teaches them a valuable lesson.

Vocabulary Boosters

This story contains several words that may be new to your class:

ingredient (noun): one of the items that goes into a mixture

whip up (verb, slang): to make or create something

proceeded (verb): moved forward with an action or activity

Discuss these words with your students and invite them to use each in a sentence.

Discussion Starters

◎ The Little Red Robin tries to convince Dog, Cat, and Duck to help her make a banana split. But they don't want to help. Is it hard to convince people to do things they don't want to do?

◎ The Little Red Robin teaches Dog, Cat, and Duck a valuable lesson. It's important to share work, so that nobody has to do all of it. What would the world be like if some people did all the work and some people did absolutely nothing?

Writing Prompts

◎ Is there something that's a special favorite of yours? It can be anything—a song or a movie or a type of food. Write about why you like this particular thing. Make your description interesting so that others will want to give it a try.

◎ Dream up a daffy dish such as gumball soup or pizza with absolutely everything. Think of as many strange ingredients as you can and write down a recipe.

-Rafunzel-
(based on "Rapunzel")

Characters

Narrator	Climber
Prince	Old Hound Dog
Mother Bird	Bumble Bee
Three Chicks	Rafunzel

Narrator: There once was a woman named Rafunzel. She was the nicest person in all the land. A wicked witch locked her away in a room at the top of a tall tower. Year after year, Rafunzel grew her blond hair until it was as long as the tower was high.

A brave prince had heard that Rafunzel was trapped in the tower. One day, the Prince rode his horse to the tower and called up to Rafunzel.

Prince: Rafunzel! Rafunzel! Throw down your hair, so I may climb your golden stair!

Narrator: Rafunzel threw down her hair. The Prince began to climb. But very soon he got tangled in a long pink ribbon.

Prince (trying to tear off the ribbon): Oh, drat!

Narrator: The Prince continued to climb up Rafunzel's long blond hair. But now the Prince was twisted in pink ribbon. Still, the Prince had heard that Rafunzel was very nice. He climbed a little higher and found that a mother bird had built a nest in Rafunzel's hair. The mother bird was tending three tiny chicks.

Mother Bird (angry): Peck, peck, peck.

Three Chicks (hungry): Chirp, chirp, chirp; chirp, chirp, chirp.

Prince (getting pecked): Ouch! Ouch! Ouch!

Narrator: The Prince escaped from the angry mother bird. He continued to climb up Rafunzel's long blond hair. But now the Prince had been pecked by a bird and was twisted in pink ribbon. Still, the Prince had heard Rafunzel was very nice and very clever. He climbed a little higher and ran into another climber, hanging on to Rafunzel's hair for dear life.

Climber: Hello, there.

Prince (surprised): Who are you?

Climber: I am a fellow climber. It is a long way to the top, I'm afraid. I have grown weary. I've stopped for a snack. Say, can I offer you a cup of tea?

Prince: Yes. That would be nice.

Climber: Jolly good. Here you are, then.

Prince (spilling the tea on his shirt): Oops! It's hard to drink tea and hang on to Rafunzel's hair at the same time.

Climber: Indeed it is, old chap, indeed it is. Well, best of luck to you.

Narrator: The Prince bid farewell to the other climber. He continued to scale Rafunzel's long blond hair. But now the Prince was soaked in tea, pecked by a bird, and twisted in pink ribbon. Still, the Prince had heard Rafunzel was very nice and very clever and very pretty. He climbed a little higher and met an old hound dog.

Old Hound Dog: Wag, wag, wag; lickety, lickety, lickety.

Prince: Good doggie. No. Good doggie. Uh… stop.

Old Hound Dog (licking the Prince's face): Slurp, slurp, slurp.

Narrator: The Prince got away from the old hound dog. He continued to climb up Rafunzel's long blond hair. But now the Prince was coated in dog slobber, soaked in tea, pecked by a bird, and twisted in pink ribbon. Still, the Prince had heard that Rafunzel was very nice and very clever and very pretty and very funny. He climbed a little higher and ran into a bumble bee, attracted by the scent of Rafunzel's luxuriant hair.

Bumble Bee: Buzz, buzz buzz. Sting! Sting! Sting!

Prince (in pain): Eek! Eyah! Argh!

Narrator: The Prince hurried away from the bumble bee. He continued to climb up Rafunzel's long blond hair. But now the Prince had one eye swollen shut from a bee sting, was coated in dog slobber, soaked in tea, pecked by a bird, and twisted in pink ribbon. Still, the Prince had heard that Rafunzel was very nice and very clever and very pretty and very funny and very good at Ping-Pong.

At last he got to the top of the tower.

Prince: Rafunzel, I am here to rescue you and take you away.

Narrator: The Prince ran to Rafunzel and bent down on one knee.

Prince: Oh, dearest Rafunzel, will you be my wife? I am a prince and we shall live in my castle and be happy together.

Rafunzel: A prince! You're a mess! You're twisted in pink ribbon. You have bird peck marks on your cheeks! There's tea all over your shirt! You have dog slobber dripping from your face! And your eye's swollen shut from a bumble bee sting!

Prince: Well, nobody's perfect. Look at you, Rafunzel! You need a haircut! Your hair is all full of ribbons and bird's nests and climbers and old hound dogs and bumble bees!

Rafunzel (furious): Well, I never!

Prince (furious): I'm outta hair. I mean… I'm outta here.

Narrator: The Prince turned to leave. But suddenly he was struck by an idea.

Prince: Hey, we may not be perfect. I'm twisted in ribbon, pecked by birds, soaked in tea, covered in dog slobber, and my eye is swollen shut from a bee sting. And your hair is full of ribbons and bird's nests and climbers and hound dogs and bumble bees. Don't you see, Rafunzel? We're perfect for each other!

I love you. Please say you'll marry me.

Rafunzel (sadly): I would, my prince. But how can we both escape from this tower?

Narrator: The Prince realized it was true. He could climb back down Rafunzel's hair. But how could they both escape together? To comfort Rafunzel, the Prince began to stroke her long blond hair.

It was then that he found yet another thing tangled in her hair. It was a key!

Prince: What's this?

Rafunzel: The key! I've been looking for that for seven years! We're free! We're free!

Narrator: The Prince and Rafunzel unlocked the door and walked down the stairs of the tower.

And so our story ends. The ribbon-tied, bird-pecked, tea-soaked, dog-slobbered, bee-stung Prince and the very nice, very clever, very pretty, very funny, and very good at Ping-Pong Rafunzel with long blond hair full of ribbons and birds nests and climbers and old hound dogs and bumble bees got married and lived happily ever after.

★the end★

-Teacher Page-

History of the Tale

"Rapunzel" is a very old folktale that for many years was simply told by one person to another. Then, in the early 1800s, it was written down for the first time by the Brothers Grimm of Germany. In their version, Rapunzel had very neat long hair. The Prince didn't encounter any bumble bees or hound dogs. But there were other challenges for the Prince. The wicked witch knew he was coming. So she cut off Rapunzel's hair and sent her away. Then the witch tied Rapunzel's hair to the top of the tower and waited for the Prince to arrive. The Prince had to battle the witch and find his true love, Rapunzel.

Vocabulary Boosters

This story contains several words that may be new to your class:

weary (adj.): tired, worn out

scale (verb): to climb up

luxuriant (adj.): rich, full, abundant

Discuss these words with your students and invite them to use each in a sentence.

Discussion Starters

◎ The Prince got twisted in ribbon, pecked by birds, soaked in tea, licked by an old hound dog, and stung by a bee. But he kept climbing. Discuss the importance of not giving up.

◎ The Prince and Rafunzel were not perfect. But they were right for each other. Is there a difference? Can you think of a situation where something wasn't perfect, but it was right for you?

Writing Prompts

◎ What other characters might the Prince encounter while climbing up Rafunzel's hair? Maybe the Prince could get caught in a storm while climbing. Write down some new twists and details you'd like to add to the story.

◎ Did the Prince and Rafunzel really live happily ever after? Did Rafunzel cut her hair? What were their kids like? Finish the story.

-The Cheetah and the Sloth-

(based on "The Tortoise and the Hare")

Characters

Sports Announcer
Sloth
Cheetah
Racing Judge

Audience featuring various animals (rabbits, squirrels, raccoons, birds)

Commercial Voice

Sports Announcer: Welcome, birds and badgers, and various other animals of the forest. We are gathered here today for the racing event of the season. Sloth has challenged Cheetah to a race. I'm down at the starting line for exclusive interviews with both racers.

My first question is for Sloth. Sloth, you're the slowest animal in the forest. Why in the world are you racing against Cheetah?

Sloth: Cheetah is always making fun of me. He's always calling me Slow Silly Sloth. I'm tired of it. So I thought I'd challenge him to a race. May the best animal win.

Sports Announcer: Interesting. Well, good luck. Now let me ask some questions of Cheetah. Cheetah, how do you feel about this race?

Cheetah: I am positively, undeniably, unquestionably the fastest animal in the world. Sloth is so slow he makes a snail look like a lightning bolt. I can run seventy miles an hour. It takes him seven hours to move one mile. You do the math!

Sports Announcer: Okay, Cheetah. You sound very confident.

Audience: (cheer, making various animal sounds such as chirps and squeaks)

Sports Announcer: The crowd is excited. The race is about to begin. Cheetah and Sloth are taking their places at the starting line. Cheetah is long and lean, with yellow spotted fur. Cheetah is wearing a pair of brand-new running shoes. Sloth is large, has brown fur, and very small eyes. Sloth is wearing a pair of brand-new shiny black shoes. They look very uncomfortable.
    Now the judge has taken his place at the starting line.

Judge: On your mark, get set, go!

Sports Announcer: And they're off!

Audience: (cheer with animal noises)

Sports Announcer: Cheetah's in the lead, streaking along at tremendous speed. Meanwhile, Sloth is moving off the starting line very slowly. In fact, I'm not even sure whether Sloth has actually started the race. Wait a minute, Sloth appears to have moved forward just slightly.
    Now back to Cheetah. Cheetah's running at incredible speed. Will you just look at that! Cheetah's already at the halfway point of the race and showing no sign of slowing down.

Audience (half): Yay, Cheetah! Go for it! Run, Cheetah, run!

Audience (half): Come on, Sloth. You can do it! Move, Sloth, move!

Sports Announcer: Wait a moment! Something extraordinary has just happened. Cheetah has stopped running. What's going on? This is amazing.

I'll describe the action. Cheetah is walking off the race track. Now Cheetah is walking into the woods. Wait… now what? Cheetah is lying down! Cheetah is lying down beneath a tree!

Birds and badgers, this is incredible. In all my years as a sportscaster I've never seen anything like it. Cheetah appears to be lying down and taking a nap.

Audience (half): C'mon, Cheetah! Get up, Cheetah, get up!

Audience (half): Faster, Sloth, faster! You can catch the Cheetah!

Sports Announcer: I am in the forest now. I have an exclusive interview with Cheetah. Cheetah, there's a question that must be on every animal's mind right now. Why have you stopped running?

Cheetah: That's simple. I'm so fast and Sloth is so slow that I thought I'd take a little nap. In fact, I think I'll take a long nap. I might even hibernate! And when I wake up, I'll still beat Sloth. Sloth is so slow he makes molasses look like a rocket ship. Well, nighty-night!

Sports Announcer: Well, there you have it. Cheetah is so confident that he will win this race that he's taking a nap. I think we will now pause for a very, very long commercial break.

Commercial Voice: Buy Big Bill's Best Boston Baked Beans! Buy Big Bill's Best Boston Baked Beans! Buy Big Bill's Best Boston Baked Beans!

Sports Announcer: We're back, live from the race between Cheetah and Sloth. Birds and badgers, this is shaping up to be an amazing race. Cheetah is in the middle of a very long nap. Meanwhile, Sloth has inched along and is drawing close to the finish line. Incredible!

Audience (half): Go, Sloth, go! You can win this race!

Audience (half): Wake up, Cheetah, wake up! Sloth is going to beat you!

Sports Announcer: I'm down near the finish line. I have an exclusive interview with Sloth, now leading this race. Sloth, do you think you have a chance to win? Do you think you can beat Cheetah?

Sloth: I'm just going to take it one step at a time. If I get to the finish line before Cheetah wakes up, well, I guess that means I'm the winner.

Sports Announcer: Incredible. Here comes Sloth, in the lead. This is quite an upset taking shape. No one ever could have predicted this outcome.

Wait a minute! Here comes a car, traveling at tremendous speed. It appears that Cheetah is driving the car. The car is heading toward the finish line.

Here comes Sloth. Here comes Cheetah. It's going to be close. And the winner is… Cheetah! Cheetah's car crossed the finish line just one second before Sloth. What a race! Cheetah is the winner!

Audience (half): Yay, Cheetah! We knew you could do it!

Audience (half): Boo, boo! That's not fair!

Judge: Quiet, quiet, please. I have an official announcement. Cheetah drove across the finish line using a car. That is against the rules. Therefore, Cheetah is disqualified for cheating. The winner of the race is Sloth.

Sports Announcer: This is just incredible, birds and badgers! I've never seen anything like it. What drama, what excitement! In all my years as a sportscaster I've never seen a race with so many surprises. Can you believe it? Sloth is the winner! Cheetah is the loser! I'll be back with a post-race wrap-up after this commercial.

Commercial Voice: Buy Big Bill's Best Boston Baked Beans! Buy Big Bill's Best Boston Baked Beans! Buy Big Bill's Best Boston Baked Beans!

Sports Announcer: We're back. And I'm talking with Sloth, the surprise winner of the race. I think there's a question on the mind of every animal right now. Sloth, how did you do it? How did you beat Cheetah?

Sloth: I never gave up, even though Cheetah started out way ahead. I just kept moving until I crossed the finish line. Slow and steady wins the race.

Sports Announcer: Amazing! So there you have it, birds and badgers. Always remember, slow and steady wins the race.

★the end★

-Teacher Page-

History of the Tale

The Cheetah and the Sloth is based on "The Tortoise and the Hare." The original is among the best known of Aesop's fables. Aesop was a Greek storyteller who lived during the sixth century B.C. His fables tend to have animals as characters. Each fable also has a moral—each one teaches a lesson about proper versus improper behavior. For example, the moral of "The Tortoise and the Hare" is that slow and steady can win in the end. Other notable Aesop's fables include "The Grasshopper and the Ant" and "The Fox and the Grapes."

Vocabulary Boosters

This story contains several words that may be new to your class:

exclusive (adj.): special; only available to one person or a small number of people

tremendous (adj.): very large or very great

disqualify (verb): to remove

Discuss these words with your students and invite them to use each in a sentence.

Discussion Starters

◎ In the story, extremely slow Sloth was able to beat very fast Cheetah. What do you think was Cheetah's mistake? Was it over-confidence? Why do you think Sloth won the race? Sloth never gave up, right?

◎ Is it better to be smart, strong, and speedy, or steady? Ask your students which quality they think is the best and why.

Writing Prompts

◎ Write a sports story. It can be a realistic story about football players or figure skaters. It can also be a wacky story about frogs playing basketball or a race between different kinds of fish.

◎ The Cheetah and the Sloth featured a sportscaster who conducted interviews. What if you could interview anyone in the world? Who would it be? Write down your questions. And write the answers that person might give.

-Little Late Riding Hood-

(based on "Little Red Riding Hood")

Characters

Mom

Narrator

Little Late Riding Hood

Tricky Monkey

Kid with Skateboard

Grandma

Narrator: There once was a young girl. She was very little and always a little late. Everywhere she went, she wore a riding coat with a hood. She was known as Little Late Riding Hood.

Mom: I've baked some banana nut bread. I want you to walk over to Grandma's house and give it to her. Now it's a bit chilly outside, so make sure and wear your riding hood. And try to be punctual.

Little Late Riding Hood: I will. I promise.

Narrator: Little Late Riding Hood walked toward Grandma's house carrying a basket of banana nut bread. Suddenly, she saw a very large monkey.

Tricky Monkey: Well, hello there little girl.

Little Late Riding Hood (a bit frightened): Hello, Mr. Monkey.

Tricky Monkey: You can drop the "Mister." Just call me Monkey. Say, where are you going with that delicious banana bread?

Little Late Riding Hood: I'm going to my grandma's house. My mom says I have to hurry.

Tricky Monkey: But it's such a beautiful day. Why don't we play hide-and-seek? I'll go first. You cover your eyes and count to one hundred. Then you can try to find me.

Little Late Riding Hood: I should hurry to Grandma's. But you're right, it is a beautiful day. Oh, why not!

Narrator: Little Late Riding Hood covered her eyes and began to count.

Little Late Riding Hood: One… two… three…

Narrator: The Tricky Monkey ran over to a boy who was riding on a skateboard.

Tricky Monkey: Hey, kid, I'll trade you my bright red mountain bike for that skateboard.

Kid: Okay.

Narrator: The Tricky Monkey jumped onto the skateboard and started skating away as fast as he could.

Kid: Hey, no fair. Where's the bike you promised? Hey! Stop, thief! Stop, Monkey!

Narrator: But the Tricky Monkey was already speeding away. Meanwhile, Little Late Riding Hood was still counting.

Little Late Riding Hood: Twenty-six… twenty-seven… twenty-eight…

Narrator: The Tricky Monkey arrived at Grandma's house. He knocked on the door and she answered.

Tricky Monkey: This is an emergency, ma'am. There has been a tornado and a hurricane spotted and an earthquake is on its way.

Grandma: Well, I don't know. It looks so sunny outside. And you're a very strange-looking young man.

Tricky Monkey: There's no time to waste, ma'am. You need to go down to the basement right away. That's the only safe place during a tornado hurricane earthquake.

Grandma: Well, all right. But I just don't know. I just don't know.

Narrator: Grandma went to the basement. The Tricky Monkey lumbered upstairs to her bedroom. He put on her pajamas and nightcap. He jumped into her bed. Meanwhile, Little Late Riding Hood was still counting.

Little Late Riding Hood: Ninety-eight… ninety-nine… one-hundred… Ready or not, Monkey, here I come.

Narrator: Suddenly, Little Late Riding Hood realized she was late to Grandma's. She didn't have time to play hide-and-go-seek with the monkey.

Little Late Riding Hood: Oh, no! Mom said not to be late to Grandma's. I lost track of time playing that silly game.

Narrator: Little Late Riding Hood ran all the way to Grandma's house. When she arrived, the door was wide open. She ran upstairs.

Little Late Riding Hood: Hi, Grandma. How are you feeling today?

Tricky Monkey (pretending to be Grandma): I feel very well, dear, thank you. Why don't you come sit down beside the bed.

Narrator: When Little Late Riding Hood sat down, she noticed how strange her grandma looked.

Little Late Riding Hood: Why, Grandma. What long hairy arms you have.

Tricky Monkey: That's from sweeping up, dear. If you sweep up your whole life your arms simply become very long and very hairy.

Little Late Riding Hood: Why, Grandma. What big ears you have.

Tricky Monkey: That's from listening to music, dear. If you listen to music your whole life your ears get very big and very weird looking.

Little Late Riding Hood: Why, Grandma. What a big funny mouth you have.

Tricky Monkey (laughing): That's for eating banana nut bread!

Narrator: With that, the Tricky Monkey reached for the banana nut bread. But just then, Grandma stepped into the room and snatched the bread away.

Grandma: Too late. No banana bread for you!

Tricky Monkey: But, but—

Grandma: Shame on you, Monkey, trying to trick an old granny. Now leave here at once or I'll call the zookeeper.

Narrator: The Tricky Monkey, still dressed in Grandma's pajamas and nightcap, ran out of the house and was never seen again.

Grandma: Little Late Riding Hood, you're right on time. Let's enjoy this banana nut bread, and I'll make us a nice cup of tea.

★the end★

-Teacher Page-

History of the Tale

The original tale features a crafty wolf. The wolf learns that Little Red Riding Hood is on the way to her grandmother's house. So the wolf runs ahead, gobbles up the grandmother, then hides in her bed waiting for Little Red Riding Hood. In most versions, the wolf gobbles her up, too. The wolf is stuffed and falls asleep. A hunter decides to check in on Grandmother. He discovers the wolf, kills him, and rescues Little Red Riding Hood and her grandmother from the wolf's stomach. This fractured version follows a similar storyline, but features a crafty monkey trying to steal some banana bread instead.

Vocabulary Boosters

This story contains several words that may be new to your class:

punctual (adj.): on time

delicious (adj.): very tasty

lumber (verb): to move in a heavy and clumsy way

Discuss these words with your students and invite them to use each in a sentence.

Discussion Starters

◎ Little Late Riding Hood got into trouble because she was running late. Is it important to be on time? Have you ever had things go wrong because you were running late?

◎ The Tricky Monkey fooled everyone: Little Late Riding Hood, the boy with the skateboard, and Grandma. But in the end, he didn't even get the banana nut bread. Is it easier for people to get what they want by being honest than by playing tricks?

Writing Prompts

◎ What do you think happened to the Tricky Monkey? Did he give the boy back his skateboard? Was he caught by the zookeeper? Or did he try to pull a new prank while dressed in Grandma's pajamas?

◎ If there's a Little Late Riding Hood, couldn't there also be a Little Speedy Riding Hood or a Little Backward Riding Hood? Think of a fun character and feature her in your own retelling of the fairy tale.

-The Ugly Woodpecker-

(based on "The Ugly Duckling")

Characters

Narrator	Danny Duck
Pa Woodpecker	Dottie Duck
Ma Woodpecker	The Ugly Woodpecker
Wilson Woodpecker (brother)	Tonya Turtle
Wilma Woodpecker (sister)	Terry Turtle

Narrator: A mother woodpecker was sitting on the three eggs in her nest. The first two eggs hatched. It was a boy and girl woodpecker. She named them Wilson and Wilma.

But the third egg would not hatch. It was larger than the other two eggs. And it was speckled, while the other two eggs were plain.

Pa Woodpecker: I think you're sitting on a robin's egg, Ma Woodpecker. Or maybe it's the egg of some other bird like a goose or a peacock.

Ma Woodpecker: Stop kidding around, Pa Woodpecker. You know good and well that this is a woodpecker egg, even if it's large and speckled.

Pa Woodpecker: Suit yourself.

Narrator: So Ma Woodpecker continued to sit on the egg. And after three long days, it began to crack. Out popped a strange creature that looked nothing like a woodpecker.

Ma Woodpecker: What a strange-looking bird.

Pa Woodpecker: My word. It has a beak like a bird. It has webbed feet, like some birds I know. But where are its wings? Where are its feathers? And what is this strange shell it has?

Wilson Woodpecker: Little brother, can you drill a hole in a tree with your beak like this: rat-a-tat-tat-tat-tat?

Narrator: The hatchling tried, but it simply hurt his beak.

Wilma Woodpecker: Little brother, can you fly like me: flap-flap-flap-flap-flap?

Narrator: The hatchling waved his arms, but he could not fly.

Wilson Woodpecker: What kind of woodpecker are you? You can't fly and you can't drill a hole with your beak.

Wilma Woodpecker: Yeah, what kind of woodpecker are you? You're the ugliest woodpecker I've ever seen.

Ma Woodpecker: Children, children, for shame!

Pa Woodpecker: Pipe down, children. I don't think this is really your little brother. I think this is a duck. We need to find a new home for him among his own kind.

Narrator: Pa Woodpecker picked up the hatchling and carried him down to the marsh. He left him with a couple of ducks named Danny and Dottie.

Danny: Who are you?

Dottie: Yes, please identify yourself.

The Ugly Woodpecker: When I was born, I thought I was a woodpecker. But now I'm told that I'm a duck.

Danny Duck: A duck, you say. Can you make sounds like this: quack, quack, quack?

The Ugly Woodpecker (tries to quack): Cough, cough, sorry.

Dottie Duck: Do you waddle when you walk?

The Ugly Woodpecker: I'm not sure. Here, I'll walk a few steps and you tell me.

Danny Duck: You have a strange way of walking. You certainly don't waddle in a cool way like a duck.

Dottie Duck: That's for sure. You don't quack and you can't waddle. I don't know what you are. You're a disgrace to ducks. I think you must actually be a very ugly woodpecker.

Danny Duck: Yeah. Those woodpeckers just wanted to get rid of you. But you're certainly not cool enough to be a duck.

Narrator: The little creature's feelings were very hurt. If this is how ducks behaved, he didn't even want to be a duck. He moved away from them just as fast as his webbed feet would carry him.

Soon, he came upon two turtles named Tonya and Terry.

Tonya Turtle: Who are you?

The Ugly Woodpecker: I don't know. I thought I was a woodpecker, but I couldn't drill holes with my beak. Then I thought maybe I was a duck. But I couldn't waddle and quack.

Tonya Turtle: No, silly, I know what you are. I was just asking who you are.

Terry Turtle: What's your name?

The Ugly Woodpecker (excited): Wait a minute. You know what I am?

Tonya Turtle: Well, you're awfully turtle-y looking. You certainly aren't a snake or an owl or a moose.

Terry Turtle: You're a turtle, no doubt about it.

The Ugly Woodpecker: A turtle. But how can you be sure?

Tonya Turtle: Well, you look exactly like us. But just to be sure, there is a simple turtle test. Can you pull your head inside your shell?

Narrator: The creature gave it a try. Sure enough, he was able to pull his head inside his shell.

Tonya Turtle: You're a turtle.

Terry Turtle: No question. You're a turtle.

The Ugly Woodpecker: I'm a turtle! I'm a turtle!

Narrator: So it was that the Ugly Woodpecker learned that he was actually a turtle. He immediately changed his name to Thaddeus T. Turtle. He was adopted by Tonya and Terry and their brothers and sisters. Thaddeus T. Turtle was always nice to other animals no matter how unusual they looked and acted. And he lived happily ever after.

★the end★

-Teacher Page-

History of the Tale

The Ugly Woodpecker is a fractured version of "The Ugly Duckling," another famous fairy tale by Hans Christian Andersen. In the original, a strange-looking bird is born into a family of ducks. The ducks don't accept him. Neither do other animals, including a cat and a hen. But the ugly duckling turns out not to be a duck at all. He grows up to be a beautiful swan.

Vocabulary Boosters

This story contains several words that may be new to your class:

speckled (adj.): covered with small spots
identify (verb): to explain what something is
disgrace (noun): an embarrassment, a shame

Discuss these words with your students and invite them to use each in a sentence.

Discussion Starters

◎ In the story, the woodpeckers and ducks did not recognize the turtle as a turtle. They thought he was some kind of ugly and strange creature. Ask your students whether people are sometimes critical of others because of a similar lack of understanding.

◎ In the story, the woodpeckers can drill holes with their beaks. Ducks can quack. Turtles can hide inside their shells. Discuss how animals have different skills and talents. Ask your students whether it's the same with people. Are some people good at sports, while others are good at math?

Writing Prompts

◎ The ducks in this story are big braggarts. Danny Duck tells the turtle, "You certainly don't waddle in a cool way like a duck." Think of some other ways animals might brag if they could talk. Write down three boasts from three different animals.

◎ *The Ugly Woodpecker* features a turtle born into a family of woodpeckers. Write about an unusual animal match up: a giraffe raised by elephants or a mouse who is friends with a cat.

-Goldilocks and the Three Bullfrogs-

(based on "Goldilocks and the Three Bears")

Characters

Narrator   Papa Bullfrog

Goldilocks   Mama Bullfrog

Baby Bullfrog

Narrator: Once upon a time, there was a family of bullfrogs. They lived in a small house at the edge of a pond. In the backyard, they had their very own swimming pool. It had three lily pads. One was for Papa Bullfrog, one for Mama Bullfrog, and one for Baby Bullfrog.

One day, the Bullfrog family was just getting ready to sit down for a meal of soup. But the soup was very hot. So they decided to go out for a short hop before their meal. By the time they returned, they expected the soup would have cooled down.

Meanwhile, a little girl named Goldilocks was walking in the woods. She noticed the little house at the edge of the pond. She went inside.

Goldilocks: Gee, three bowls of soup. I wonder who these belong to?

Narrator: Goldilocks took a spoonful from Papa Bullfrog's bowl. But before she took a sip, she noticed that something was strange.

Goldilocks: There are flies in this soup. Yuck!

Narrator: Then she took a spoonful of Mama Bullfrog's soup. But before she put it in her mouth, she again noticed that something was odd.

Goldilocks: This soup is full of crickets. Ugh!

Narrator: Then Goldilocks noticed that Baby Bullfrog's soup didn't have any flies or crickets.

Goldilocks: This soup is just right. Mmmmmm.

Narrator: Goldilocks ate all of Baby Bullfrog's soup. Then she looked out the window and noticed the frogs' swimming pool. She thought it would be nice to take a swim.

Goldilocks swam for a while. She noticed that there were three lily pads in the pool. This was strange. She wondered who lived in this house. It looked like it would be fun to sit on one of the lily pads.

Goldilocks climbed up on Papa Bullfrog's lily pad.

Goldilocks: This lily pad is too big.

Narrator: Goldilocks dove back into the water and swam to Mama Bullfrog's lily pad.

Goldilocks: This lily pad is too slippery.

Narrator: She swam over to the third and final lily pad, which belonged to Baby Bullfrog.

Goldilocks: This lily pad is just right.

Narrator: Suddenly, there was a strange burbling noise. The lily pad was sinking. Goldilocks fell into the water with a splash. Then she swam to the edge of the pool and got out.

Goldilocks decided to go back inside the house for a look around. She walked upstairs. The first thing she noticed was a very bouncy-looking bed. Who lived in a house with fly soup, lily pads in the pool, and bouncy beds?

Goldilocks climbed onto Papa Bullfrog's bed and began to bounce. She immediately flew high into the air and nearly bumped her head on the ceiling.

Goldilocks: This bed is too bouncy.

Narrator: Next she tried out Mama Bullfrog's bed. She hopped once and nothing happened. She hopped again and still nothing happened.

Goldilocks: This bed is not bouncy enough.

Narrator: So Goldilocks began to jump on Baby Bullfrog's bed. It was perfect. She could bounce higher and higher, then lower and lower. She could do flips and flops and tricks.

Goldilocks: Wheee! Woooo! Wheeehaaaa!

Narrator: After a while, Goldilocks grew tired of bouncing on Baby Bullfrog's bed. She lay down and went to sleep.

Soon, the Bullfrog family came hopping back from their outing. They were hungry and looking forward to some tasty soup full of flies and crickets. Suddenly, Papa Bullfrog noticed that something was not quite right.

Papa Bullfrog: Ribbit, someone's been sampling my soup.

Mama Bullfrog: Someone also took a spoonful of my soup, ribbit.

Baby Bullfrog: Ribbit, ribbit, ribbit, someone ate my soup. Now it's all gone.

Narrator: Then the three bullfrogs noticed that something was different about their swimming pool.

Papa Bullfrog: Someone's been sitting on my lily pad, ribbit.

Mama Bullfrog: Ribbit, someone has definitely been sitting on my lily pad.

Baby Bullfrog: Someone sat on my lily pad. And it sank, ribbit, ribbit, ribbit.

Narrator: The three hopped upstairs.

Papa Bullfrog: Someone's been bouncing… ribbit… on my bed.

Mama Bullfrog: Yes, there's definitely been… ribbit… someone bouncing on my bed.

Baby Bullfrog: Someone has been bouncing on my bed. And she's still there, ribbit, ribbit, ribbit.

With all the commotion, Goldilocks woke up. She was greeted by a family of frogs staring at her. They were hopping mad. Goldilocks got out of bed and jumped out the window, just like a frog. Then she ran out of the woods, and never snuck into a strange house again.

★the end★

-Teacher Page-

History of the Tale

Goldilocks and the Three Bullfrogs is based on the classic "Goldilocks and the Three Bears." In the original, Goldilocks wanders into a house belonging to three bears. She tries their porridge, sits in their chairs, and sleeps in their beds. When the bears find her, she wakes with a fright and runs away. Both the original and fractured versions are meant to be fun, but also are meant to teach a couple of important lessons. First, people shouldn't interfere with nature. Second, people should not sneak into the homes of strangers.

Vocabulary Boosters

This story contains several words that may be new to your class:

odd (adj.): strange, unusual

outing (noun): a walk or a trip

commotion (noun): a noisy disturbance

Discuss these words with your students and invite them to use each in a sentence.

Discussion Starters

◎ What if animals actually lived in houses? What would those houses be like? The Bullfrog family had bouncy beds and a swimming pool with lily pads.

What types of things might you find in the homes of giraffes, penguins, skunks, and other animals?

◎ Was it wrong for Goldilocks to wander around in the Bullfrog family's home? What do you think this story—and the original Goldilocks—are really about? Do the stories, perhaps, teach lessons about being careful not to disturb the homes of animals in nature?

Writing Prompts

◎ There's the original tale, "Goldilocks and the Three Bears." And there's the new version you just read: Goldilocks and the Three Bullfrogs. Write your own Goldilocks story. It can feature three chimps, four dinosaurs, or whatever else you dream up.

◎ In this story, frogs always say "ribbit." But what about snakes? Maybe talking snakes would use lots of hissing "s" words: "Sssooo sssorry, sssir." And maybe owls would ask a lot of questions: "Who is there?" "Who is coming to dinner?" Write a conversation between a frog, a snake, and an owl. If you like, add in other talking animals as well.

-Slurping Beauty-
(based on "Sleeping Beauty")

Characters

Narrator	Prince Charming
Wicked Fairy	Slurping Beauty
King	Prince Alarming

Narrator: Once upon a time, there lived a king in a faraway land. He had one daughter, a lovely young princess. He decided to throw her a feast for her tenth birthday. It was a wonderful feast, and he invited all the good fairies from the surrounding woodlands.

Each good fairy cast a different spell on the young princess. One spell made her sweet. Another spell made her smart. Another spell made her pretty. But there was one particular fairy—a Wicked Fairy—who had not been invited to the feast. The Wicked Fairy grew angry and cast a curse on the Princess.

Wicked Fairy: Zarsasee Zorsesee Zizzle and Zoup.
You're manners will be frightful. You'll slurp up your soup.

Narrator: The King was horrified. He immediately issued a proclamation to try to keep the curse against his daughter from coming true.

King: All spoons throughout the kingdom must be destroyed at once. Citizens of the land, gather up any and all bowls. Take them to the royal dump immediately. From this point forward, soup is outlawed in my kingdom. No more clam chowder, no more chicken and stars. Hear me, hear me, by royal proclamation, there is to be no more soup.

Narrator: A few years later, the Princess had her sixteenth birthday. The King arranged a huge feast. Prince Charming, from a neighboring land, was to be the guest of honor. He was famous the whole world over for his fine breeding. The King had even hired a new cook specifically for the occasion.

Prince Charming (snobbily): I would like to say a few words to the lovely Princess. If her manners are anything like my manners—ahem, ahem—I am sure we will get along quite splendidly.

Narrator: The waiters began to serve the meal. To the King's horror, they set down bowls of soup. The King had completely forgotten to tell the new cook that soup was forbidden throughout the land.

Slurping Beauty: I've never tasted such a delight before. What is this fine food?

Prince Charming: Why, it's soup, of course.

King: Oh, no. It's soup!

Slurping Beauty: It's delicious. I've never tasted anything so delicious. Slurp, slurp, slurp.

Prince Charming: Well, I never. I believe that I must be going at once. I have a previous engagement that completely slipped my mind. King, thank you for a most charming evening. Your daughter is a most… interesting young lady.

Narrator: The King was furious that the feast had gone so badly. The Wicked Fairy's curse had taken hold. Slurping Beauty had scared off Prince Charming with her terrible manners. Sure, Prince Charming was something of a snob. But what about the next young man who came to dinner? What if Slurping Beauty scared him off, too?

The King decided he would fire the new cook at once. But Slurping Beauty begged him not to. Until now, she had never tasted soup. And she loved it.

Slurping Beauty: Please, Daddy. Don't fire the cook. Have him make more soup. I love it. Slurp, slurp, slurp.

Narrator: The King could not deny his daughter. And so began a period of Slurping Beauty trying all the soup she'd missed out on throughout her childhood. Night after night, meal after meal, she tried different soups—split pea, chicken noodle, beef and barley. She loved them all. And she slurped them all up.

The old King was terribly upset. If his daughter kept behaving this way, she might never find a husband. It so happened that another prince was passing through the land. The King had no choice but to invite Prince Alarming to dinner.

Soup was served as usual. The King expected that it was going to be a very embarrassing evening.

Prince Alarming: I would like to tell a riddle to the lovely Princess. What did the flower say to the bee? Buzz off! Get it? Buzz off!

Narrator: The Princess began to laugh. And then Prince Alarming began to laugh. He had a goofy high-pitched laugh that sounded like this:

Prince Alarming: Hee-har, hee-har, hee-har.

Slurping Beauty: Slurp, slurp, slurp.

Prince Alarming: Knock, knock.

Slurping Beauty: Who's there? Slurp, slurp, slurp.

Prince Alarming: Lettuce.

Slurping Beauty: Lettuce who? Slurp, slurp, slurp.

Prince Alarming: Let us alone! Get it? Let us alone!!!

Narrator: Slurping Beauty laughed so hard that soup came out her nose. That made Prince Alarming laugh even harder: hee-har, hee-har, hee-har.

Slurping Beauty didn't mind Prince Alarming's goofy laugh. In fact, she thought it was cute. Prince Alarming didn't mind the way Slurping Beauty ate her soup. "She has a healthy appetite," he would say, always with a hearty laugh: "Hee-har, hee-har, hee-har."

The two rather enjoyed one another's funny habits. They fell in love and lived happily ever after.

★the end★

-Teacher Page-

History of the Tale

"Sleeping Beauty" is a traditional folktale that has been retold countless times over the years. Whatever the version, the story always features a princess who is the victim of a curse. If she pricks her finger on a spindle—a type of pin used with a spinning wheel—she will fall asleep for a hundred years. The King and Queen order that all spindles be removed from the kingdom. But she still manages to find one. Sure enough, she pricks her finger and falls asleep for a hundred years. Finally, a handsome prince awakens her from the spell. This version follows a similar but fractured story line: the Princess must never eat soup. If she does, she'll never get a date. An effort is made to remove all the bowls and soup spoons from the kingdom, but to no avail.

Vocabulary Boosters

This story contains several words that may be new to your class:

proclamation (noun): an official announcement
alarming (adj.): shocking and surprising
breeding (noun): behavior and manners that are the result of the way a person is raised

Discuss these words with your students and invite them to use each in a sentence.

Discussion Starters

◎ Prince Charming had perfect manners. But he and Slurping Beauty did not get along. Prince Alarming told silly jokes and had a goofy laugh. He and Slurping Beauty got along great. Ask your students about choosing friends. Is it important to follow one's heart, no matter what others may think?

◎ The Wicked Fairy's curse was supposed to keep Slurping Beauty from ever getting a date. But Slurping Beauty found a way around the curse. Discuss with your students whether it's possible to fix most situations, even if they seem bad at first.

Writing Prompts

◎ Write a royal proclamation. Your proclamation can be serious, demanding that people stop littering, for example. Or it can be a silly one, banning people from wearing the color red, say. Whatever type of proclamation you write, use lots of fancy language such as "Hear ye, hear ye."

◎ Prince Alarming loved silly jokes and riddles. Make up at least three of them that will be guaranteed to make him laugh "hee-har, hee-har, hee-har."